The American Revolution

LANCASTER PAMPHLETS

The American Revolution

M. J. Heale

METHUEN · LONDON

First published in 1986 by
Methuen & Co. Ltd
11 New Fetter Lane
London EC4P 4EE

© 1986 M. J. Heale

Typeset in Great Britain by
Scarborough Typesetting Services
and printed by
Richard Clay (The Chaucer Press)
Bungay, Suffolk

British Library Cataloguing in Publication Data

Heale, M. J.
The American Revolution. – (Lancaster pamphlets)
1. United States – History – Revolution
I. Title   II. Series
973.3   E208

ISBN 0–416–38910–4

Contents

Foreword

Lancaster Pamphlets offer concise and up-to-date accounts of major historical topics, primarily for the help of students preparing for Advanced Level examinations, though they should also be of value to those pursuing introductory courses in universities and other institutions of higher education. They do not rely on prior textbook knowledge. Without being all-embracing, their aims are to bring some of the central themes or problems confronting students and teachers into sharper focus than the textbook writer can hope to do; to provide the reader with some of the results of recent research which the textbook may not embody; and to stimulate thought about the whole interpretation of the topic under discussion.

At the end of this pamphlet is a list of the recent or fairly recent works that the writer considers most relevant to the subject.

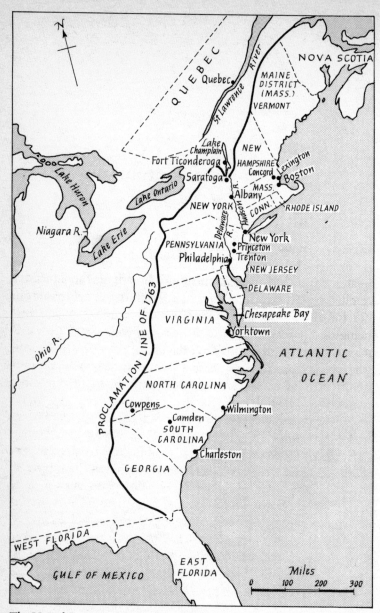

The United States in the war for independence.

Even this is rather a narrow view of the revolutionary process, but it again recognizes that a revolution is not the same thing as a war for independence. A colony may secure its independence from a mother country by war or by agreement without experiencing a revolution. Definitions of revolution vary, but they normally assume that far-reaching change must occur *within* the country concerned. Some scholars have, in fact, denied that there was an American Revolution, only an act of secession from the British Empire, but most agree that a revolution did occur, or perhaps a series of revolutions – political, constitutional, ideological and social.

The recognition that the American Revolution consisted in more than a struggle for independence, that it included fundamental social and political change within America, raises another question: how long did it last? It might be agreed, for the sake of argument, that the Battle of Lexington of 1775 or the Declaration of Independence of 1776 marked the beginning of the revolution, but what marked the end? The Treaty of Paris of 1783 formally ended the war, but it took several more years for Americans to sort out their system of government. The celebrated American Constitution was drawn up in Philadelphia in 1787 and it went into operation in 1789. Should the adoption of the Constitution mark the conclusion of the American Revolution? By the 1780s a number of American states, like Pennsylvania and Vermont, were experimenting with some very radical styles of government, which to them represented the unfolding of the revolutionary logic, but some constraint was put on these state governments by the new American Constitution. Did that Constitution then represent the culmination of the American Revolution, or was it rather a counter-revolutionary measure, as some historians have argued? Should the American Revolution be regarded as over, successfully or not, when George Washington was safely installed as the first President in 1789? For many Americans at the time the revolution was still in its infancy, and they continued to fall out with one another over the shape their republic should take for at least another generation. In the years after 1789 Americans added flesh and blood to the bare bones of their Constitution in the form of new taxes, a reconstituted national debt, the building of a capital city to be called

Washington, the creation of political parties, and the establishment of a host of institutions and customs not mentioned by the Constitution but essential to stable government. In 1812 war again broke out with Britain, and the ending of that war in 1815, after the United States had demonstrated to itself and to the world that its new system of government had withstood both internal strains and external attack, could again be said to mark the culmination of the American Revolution.

But in a sense the American Revolution has never ended. The Declaration of Independence declares that 'all men are created equal', and ever since 1776 those Americans who have felt that they were not being treated as equals have demanded their rights. The women's suffrage movement, for example, was based in part on the demand that the promise of the American Revolution be fulfilled. In recent years American blacks and women in particular have invoked the Declaration of Independence in their own campaigns for equal rights, as have other minority groups, like Hispanics, gays and the elderly. In this sense, the American Revolution remains to be completed.

The view from Britain

On 19 April 1775 British troops encountered a group of Massachusetts militiamen at Lexington. Suddenly a shot rang out, both sides opened fire, and the War for Independence had begun. It has always been unclear who fired that first shot but, as Ralph Waldo Emerson was later to write, it was a 'shot heard round the world'. These American colonists were British subjects and had taken up arms against the soldiers of their king. Within a few years their revolt would turn into a successful revolution, the first of those revolutions of modern history directed against a hereditary monarch and a traditional regime. The shot that was heard round the world was still echoing in France in 1789, in various European capitals in 1848, even in Russia in 1917.

Why did British troops and American militiamen come to blows? The American rebels themselves had no difficulty in answering this question. Time and again the revolutionary leaders explained that they had resisted because the British government was trying to enslave them. Several months before the skirmish at Lexington one worried American wrote: 'I speak it with grief – I speak it with anguish – Britons are our oppressors: I speak it with shame – I speak it with indignation – WE ARE SLAVES.' To understand the origins of the revolutionary war it is necessary to understand this mentality, to understand why it was that so many Americans had come to believe that Britain was trying to reduce them to slavery. This American outlook will be discussed more fully on pp. 13–23, but as proof of their charges colonial leaders pointed to the behaviour of British governments in the years after the Seven Years War. It was the policies and measures of British ministers between about 1763 and 1775 which caused Americans to fear for their liberties. Why, then, did the king's governments undertake actions so disruptive of Anglo-American accord?

In the eyes of George III and his ministers, of course, there was little in the British measures which should have occasioned such violent colonial alarm. The Americans objected in particular to the taxes that the British governments attempted to levy on them, but these taxes were very light when compared to those in Britain, and the money raised was intended to pay part of the high costs of colonial defence and administration. It was not even as if these taxes had been high-handedly imposed, like those that Charles I had tried to thrust on his subjects in the seventeenth century; they were properly introduced by Acts of Parliament, and Parliament was the supreme governing body in the British Empire. To many people in Britain it seemed as if the American colonists, who for the most part enjoyed a relatively high standard of living, were selfishly refusing to contribute even a modest amount to the costs of their own defence. To the most rigid of British minds, the American war, when it came, was little more than a vulgar exercise in tax evasion.

The American revolt, of course, cannot be explained in such crass terms. The British ministries themselves knew perfectly well that colonial resistance could not be dismissed as contemptuously as that. The proposed taxes were light when compared with those in Britain, but there were other restrictions on the colonies which limited their opportunities for maximizing wealth. Since the mid-seventeenth century, for example, colonial trade had been regulated by the Navigation Laws, which required that some colonial products be exported directly to England, and only in English or colonial ships, and it could be argued that it was unfair to impose taxes on top of such commercial restraints. Indeed, this was one reason why George III's ministers did not attempt to introduce heavier colonial taxes than they did, but they believed that it was reasonable to raise some revenue from the colonies, particularly when they intended to spend it in the colonies. However, taxation was not the only and not the most important issue in dispute between Britain and her American colonies in the fifteen years before the Declaration of Independence. Friction between the two first seriously emerged when the British ministries attempted to make changes in the government and administration of the British Empire. It was this adoption, in the 1760s, of a policy of imperial reorganization which triggered off the sequence of events leading to the War for Independence.

A new imperial policy had been made necessary by the Seven Years War and by the decades of neglect of the empire before that. British settlement of North America had been taking place somewhat erratically since 1607, and by 1750 there were thirteen British colonies scattered along the Atlantic seaboard, and more in the islands of the Caribbean. The British, however, were not the only nation to penetrate the American continent, for Spain possessed Florida and a large part of the south-west, while France claimed Canada and much of the interior. Competition for the riches of the continent led to the outbreak of hostilities between Britain and France in 1754, which merged with the war in Europe of 1756–63. Britain emerged from that war with a vastly increased empire, not least in North America, where France surrendered all her possessions and Spain agreed to withdraw from Florida. She also emerged with her national debt doubled to an alarming sum of over £130 million. Contributing to this debt was the cost of the war in North America, which for the most part the colonies had escaped paying for, although they greatly benefited from the removal of their French rivals.

Britain's victory in the Seven Years War may have made her the world's greatest power, but when George Grenville became the king's chief minister in 1763 he was confronted by almost insuperable problems. His fundamental task was that of governing this far-flung empire, parts of which had been accustomed to French or Spanish rule. Quite apart from the thirteen existing North American colonies, Britain now had to do something with her new responsibilities in Canada, the Floridas and the American interior. The thirteen colonies needed attention too, for in the years of neglect they had often evaded imperial regulations and ignored the requests of British governments. Some of the elected assemblies, which colonists liked to regard as their equivalents to Parliament, were trying to exercise powers once held by the royal governors. And it was not only disrespectful assemblies which worried the king's ministers. Over the years the British government had signed treaties with a number of Indian tribes, and these treaties sometimes needed to be enforced against the ambitions of various groups of colonists. Claims to land were a perennial problem for imperial officials, for land in North America could be variously claimed by sundry colonial governments, land companies, individuals and Indian tribes. Colonial trade was another issue demanding the scrutiny of imperial officials, not least the lucrative fur trade of the interior and of Canada. All these problems and more jostled for the attention of George Grenville and his colleagues as they considered how best to govern Britain's newly extended empire.

This empire had somehow to be occupied, administered and defended, not an easy task in times when communications were slow and armies small. It was one thing for Parliament to pass a law and quite another to have it enforced in a distant land. The urgency of providing for colonial defence was made clear in the spring and summer of 1763, when the Ottawa chief, Pontiac, led a major Indian rising in which all but two of the British posts west of Niagara were destroyed. The Pontiac conspiracy confirmed the view already held in London that the colonies were unable or unwilling adequately to provide for their own defence.

In October the ministry issued what became known as the Proclamation of 1763, which attempted both to provide for the government of the new American territories and to deal with the Indian problem. The proclamation created two new provinces in East and West Florida, under separate governments, and in Canada the new colony of Quebec was established to administer the recent acquisitions in that area. An important provision of the proclamation was that setting the boundary of white settlement along the watershed of the Appalachians, at least for the time being. This, it was hoped, would preserve the interior for the tribes, minimize white–Indian conflict and encourage white settlement along the eastern seaboard and in the new colonies in Canada and the Floridas. From London this check on western settlement seemed rational and humane, but it outraged many frontiersmen and land speculators. The plan also involved putting the west under military control, and colonists were not slow to realize that, however much keeping the peace on the frontier necessitated a standing army, that army could one day be turned against them.

As the Grenville ministry was unfolding its plans for governing North America, it was also seeking ways of defraying the costs involved. No one was more aware than George Grenville that administering and defending these vast territories would cost a lot of money. In theory this money might be raised in Britain, but the British public debt was already at a disturbingly high level, thanks to the Seven Years War, as was the country's tax burden. Grenville did in fact increase British taxes, although a new tax on cider produced rioting in the south of England. It was estimated that the cost of keeping a regular army on the American mainland alone would be £200,000 a year. These troops were necessary to defend the American colonies from the Indians (and to defend Indians from colonists), and to deter the European powers from returning. Yet the colonies themselves were now relatively prosperous and, according to one estimate, the average American paid a mere six pence a year in taxes while the average taxpayer at home paid twenty-five shillings. Grenville did not expect to be able to make the colonies pay for all the costs of their defence, but he thought it reasonable to expect them to pay a part.

Hence he embarked on a policy which had fateful consequences. Existing Acts of Parliament which put customs duties on goods entering the colonies were more vigorously enforced, to the annoyance of American merchants. In 1764 Grenville secured the Sugar Act (or the Plantation Act), a complex measure which in fact reduced the duty on foreign molasses imported by the New England rum distillers. This reduced the incentive to smuggle, thus obliging many American merchants to pay the duty for the first time and to respect other customs regulations. As a revenue measure, however, this did not raise much money, and in 1765 Grenville tried for the first time to impose an internal tax on the colonies with the Stamp Act. Stamp duties had been levied in England for over seventy years, and the ministry wished to extend the same principle to the colonies with a tax on newspapers, playing cards, legal documents, liquor licenses, insurance policies, ships' papers and the like. These levies were to be somewhat lighter than those in Britain, the money raised would be spent in the colonies, and even then it would be little more than a quarter of the sum needed for colonial defence. It was a modest enough measure in the eyes of the ministry, which failed fully to anticipate the constitutional issues it would stir up. Already a few colonial assemblies had complained that the Sugar Act meant that they were being taxed without their consent. The imposition of a new internal tax by Parliament raised even more starkly the issue of whether the American colonists could be taxed by a body in which they were not directly represented.

The colonial reaction to the various measures of the Grenville ministry, particularly to the Stamp Act, was extraordinarily intense. The Sugar Act had mainly disturbed New Englanders, but the Stamp Act was resented throughout the colonies, not least by influential citizens like lawyers, merchants, printers and planters, whose business activities were directly affected by the new duties. The Rhode Island assembly voiced a popular refrain when it pointed out that men who were taxed on the whim of others 'cannot possibly have any property . . . but are indeed reduced to the most abject slavery'. Secret organizations known as the Sons of Liberty sprang up in the main towns to co-ordinate resistance and to threaten those who upheld the law. All the stamp distributors were forced to resign their offices. Merchants formed non-importation associations to boycott British goods. In

October 1765 nine colonies sent representatives to a Stamp Act Congress, held in New York, and while it insisted on its loyalty to the king it also insisted that colonists enjoyed the same rights as Englishmen at home and could be taxed only by their own representative assemblies.

The British government did not agree with these constitutional objections but it was powerless in the face of the widespread resistance to its measures. The army for which it was trying to raise money was meant primarily to man the frontier forts; it could not be used to subdue whole colonies. If no one was prepared to be a stamp distributor in the colonies the stamp duties could not be levied. Further, the American disturbances prompted some influential interests in Britain to question the wisdom of the measures which had provoked them. Worried by the trade boycott and the prospect of a loss of debts owed to them, British merchants urged Parliament to repeal the Stamp Act. By this time the Grenville ministry had been replaced by one headed by Lord Rockingham (for reasons unrelated to American matters) and, unable to impose its will on the colonies, the ministry secured the repeal of the Act in March 1766. But at the same time Parliament passed the Declaratory Act asserting Parliament's right to make laws for the colonies 'in all cases whatsoever'. The British government thus abandoned a measure it could not enforce but it was not abandoning the constitutional principle of parliamentary sovereignty.

British ministers were also reluctant to abandon altogether the effort to raise a revenue from the American colonies. Another change of government brought the brilliant and unstable Charles Townshend to the Treasury as Chancellor of the Exchequer. Parliament was still restive at the high level of taxation in Britain, the cost of providing for colonial defence was found to be higher than ever, and the colonies were still escaping much of a contribution. Townshend determined on another attempt at raising money from the colonies, and his Revenue Act of 1767 imposed duties on the colonial import of tea and a number of manufactured goods, notably glass, paint and paper. There was some precedent for external taxes of this kind, and it was hoped that they would prove less provocative than internal taxes like stamp duties, although many colonists had made clear their opposition to both forms of taxation. As important was a provision in the Townshend measures creating an American civil list – that is, the money raised need not after all be spent on defence, but could be used to pay for the salaries of governors, judges and other royal officials, who would no longer be dependent on the colonial assemblies for income. Townshend also established at Boston an American Board of Customs Commissioners, directly responsible to Britain, and allowed colonial courts to issue writs of assistance, enabling customs officials to search homes and stores. In the past imperial policy had often been frustrated by the resistance of the colonial assemblies, but now an administrative machinery seemed to be in the making which would by-pass these obstreperous bodies.

Colonial resistance to the Townshend Acts developed more slowly than had been the case with Grenville's measures, but none the less it once again became determined and widespread. The Americans reiterated their claims that only their assemblies could tax the colonies. Another trade boycott on imports from Britain was organized, there were sporadic outbreaks of rioting and customs officers were subjected to intimidation. The assaults on customs officers prompted the ministry in 1768 to send troops and warships to Boston, where their presence became a source of resentment to local citizens. In March 1770 this friction erupted into the so-called Boston Massacre, in which five Bostonians were killed. By this time, in fact, a new British government headed by Lord North had already accepted the need to abandon the un-enforceable Townshend policy, which was costing more money than it was raising, and in what was intended as one last concession the ministry repealed all the duties, retaining only that on tea 'as a mark of the supremacy of Parliament'. The immediate crisis again receded, but the decision to keep the tea duty meant that the constitutional issue had not been finally resolved.

The collapse of the trade boycott coincided with the return of prosperity in the colonies, and it looked for a time as if the American troubles might be over. But this was an illusion. Colonists smuggled in foreign tea rather than pay the duty on British tea, and disruptive incidents did occasionally occur.

Customs officers and other imperial officials continued to find it difficult to enforce the law. In 1772 the Royal Navy schooner *Gaspée* was burned by Rhode Islanders when it ran aground, and Americans throughout the colonies were disturbed when the British government proposed that anyone suspected of the offence be tried in England. Late in the same year Governor Hutchinson of Massachusetts revealed that he and the senior Massachusetts judges were to receive their salaries direct from the crown, payable from the tea duties. Interpreting these and other moves as evidence of a design to impose arbitrary rule from Britain, American radicals formed committees of correspondence in several colonies to liaise with one another and circulate anti-British propaganda.

As opposition to British pretensions was being co-ordinated in the colonies, the North ministry was grappling with a severe financial crisis in Britain. The East India Company in particular, which had so successfully exploited the commercial opportunities of the Indian sub-continent, was hard hit by this panic, and the mountains of unsold tea that were piling up in its warehouses were made the larger by the American refusal to buy British tea. Lord North's response was the Tea Act of 1773, which permitted the company to sell tea directly to North America, with a remission of the customs duties paid in Britain. This should have had the effect of reducing the price of tea in America, thus making it unprofitable to smuggle foreign tea and ensuring that the remaining Townshend duty be paid. Further, the East India Company was allowed to appoint its own agents in the colonies to sell the tea. The Tea Act excited little comment in Britain, but it was widely opposed in America, where the principle of parliamentary taxation had long been resisted and where merchants who had been smuggling Dutch tea would presumably suffer a loss of business. This renewed attempt to raise a revenue from the colonies and to control their trade could only deepen American suspicions about the thrust of British policy, and merchants and radicals in all the major ports coalesced in open defiance. In Philadelphia, New York and Charleston the tea agents, like the stamp distributors before them, were forced to resign their offices by the local citizenry. When the tea arrived, some ports sent it back to Britain. In Boston, where Governor Hutchinson attempted to persuade the tea agents to accept the tea, the *impasse* was broken when men disguised as Mohawk Indians dumped the tea chests into the harbour. This was the celebrated Boston Tea Party of December 1773. It demonstrated that, by this date, the imperial authorities were powerless in Boston, as indeed they were in at least three other colonial cities.

The North ministry had intended its repeal of most of the Townshend duties in 1770 to be the last government concession to American demands, and besides it could hardly countenance the kind of insubordination which had occurred in Boston without abdicating its authority completely. Concluding that Boston was at the centre of colonial troubles, the ministry decided to isolate and punish it. By the Coercive (or Intolerable) Acts of 1774 the port of Boston was closed until obedience had been restored; the rights of the Massachusetts' assembly were reduced, and the governor was given the power to appoint all judges, sheriffs and magistrates and to forbid the holding of town meetings. At about the same time the commander-in-chief in America, General Thomas Gage, was made the new Governor of Massachusetts, which thus seemed to be subjected to a form of military rule. Another measure of 1774, although it had been planned earlier, was the Quebec Act, which put much of the area to the north-west of the Ohio river under the province of Quebec, gave full recognition to Roman Catholicism, placed authority in the hands of a governor without an elected assembly, left French civil law in force and limited trial by jury. This attempt to provide for the administration of Canada, like the Coercive Acts, seemed to betray an intent to put North America under authoritarian forms of government.

These several Acts of 1774 looked to many Americans like a concerted assault on their liberties. Instead of isolating Massachusetts and subduing the malcontents, the measures resulted in widespread resistance. Colonial assemblies, town and county meetings, newspapers, clergymen and other men of influence, denounced the actions of the British government. In September 1774, following a proposal of the Massachusetts assembly, a Congress met in Philadelphia consisting of representatives from twelve colonies. The Continental Congress, while not yet calling for independence, did deny that the colonies were subject to the authority of Parliament. The king's American subjects, according to the Congress, like Englishmen at home, possessed the rights 'to life, liberty and property', and only their own legislatures could enact 'all the cases of taxation and internal polity', subject to the veto of the crown. To further this claim to colonial self-government the Congress endorsed yet another boycott of British goods. The British government could not yield on the issue of the sovereign authority of Parliament, and in February 1775 Parliament declared Massachusetts to be in a state of rebellion. The military governor of the colony, General Gage, prepared for combat, and in April the fateful encounter at Lexington occurred.

The view from America

After 1763 the British ministries' attempts to provide for the government of the empire brought them into conflict with the American colonies. Not all their measures were well conceived, but perhaps more surprising than their periodic irritation at colonial obstinacy was their forbearance. The successive British ministers, after all, acted throughout in a manner consistent with their understanding of the English constitution, in which Parliament was the supreme governing body in the British Empire. Yet they did not immediately rush to arms when their authority was defied. Quite apart from anything else, they were well aware of the extraordinary difficulty of enforcing their will in distant colonies, and when one measure did not work they usually tried another. With the advantage of hindsight it may be questioned whether the British ministries' willingness to yield and to experiment was altogether wise, for what seemed reasonable behaviour to them acquired a distinctly sinister character in American eyes. To many leading colonists the erratic measures of the British government seemed like successive steps to deprive them of their liberty, perhaps even a concerted conspiracy to overthrow the celebrated English constitution itself.

The American colonists, no less than the British ministries, acted on the conviction that right was on their side. The colonial leaders had their own understanding of the English constitution and of the rights and privileges it conferred on the king's subjects

13

throughout his empire. In their view it was the British authorities who were guilty of unconstitutional and unlawful acts. Where the British government saw a set of unruly and insolent colonists rising in rebellion to further their selfish or misguided interests, the colonists saw a corrupt British ministry steadily extending its power over them and bent on reducing them to no less a state than slavery.

The colonists were not really using exaggerated language when they accused the British ministers of trying to turn them into slaves. In the political language of the eighteenth century the opposite of freedom was slavery, and anything which reduced a man's liberties brought him closer to slavery. When Patrick Henry shouted, as he probably did, 'Give me liberty or give me death', he was saying that even the prospect of death was sweeter than the prospect of 'chains and slavery'. If the colonists submitted to the absolute claims of Parliament, argued a lawyer from North Carolina, then they became dependent, 'not the condition of free men, but of slaves'. The word slavery was widely used by Americans to describe the status to which the British government apparently intended to reduce them. The 'acts and measures . . . adopted since the last war', complained the colonial leaders when they met together in the Continental Congress, 'demonstrate a system formed to enslave America'.

To understand why the Americans rebelled, then, it is necessary to understand why they saw the measures of the British ministries after 1763 as designed to make them slaves. They did so in part because the colonies were no longer primitive settlements struggling for physical survival. Over the years relatively complex social structures had developed in most colonies, hierarchical orders in which social élites, for the most part born and bred in America, regarded themselves as the natural rulers of colonial society. These wealthy planters, landowners and merchants were not aristocrats in the British sense, but they did constitute a gentry class wielding considerable social and political influence. The colonial gentry, furthering their interests in the assemblies, articulated an ideology which owed a great deal to English constitutional thought and which emphasized the rights and liberties of free-born Englishmen and the limitations on royal power. Any king who sought to

14

enlarge that power could be accused of seeking to enslave his subjects. But it was not only ideological considerations which swayed colonial leaders. They had economic interests, too, and it was when they were suffering from financial reverses that issues of constitutional principle seemed to have most pertinence. Further, the colonial élites did not resist Britain on their own. In the 1760s and 1770s many men of humbler rank – artisans, tradesmen, seamen, small farmers and others – also actively resisted British demands, often because they too saw those measures as striking both at their economic interests and at their constitutional liberties. The colonial gentry and ordinary people frequently agreed after 1763 that Britain threatened all Americans with what could be termed slavery. And as Americans of all ranks were induced by both ideological and economic considerations to espy a sinister intent in British policy, one extraordinary domestic circumstance rendered slavery peculiarly fearful to them. The fact was that slaves did exist in all thirteen American colonies, and although they were black their presence served as a vivid and constant reminder to white colonists of the dreadful fate that awaited men who could not preserve their liberties.

One reason for the alarm provoked in the American colonies by British measures, then, was that these measures were viewed through the eyes of gentlemen well versed in the libertarian principles of the idealized English constitution. The well-to-do merchants, lawyers, landowners and planters who enjoyed high status in colonial society had long sought to exert influence in the political institutions which had been established in each colony, such as the governor's council and especially the assembly. The assemblies were elected by the colonists themselves, at least by those with enough property to vote, which was usually a very large number, and over the years the assemblies gained in power as they modelled themselves on the House of Commons. While wishing to remain loyal to the king, the colonists naturally sought a measure of self-government, and the élites who sat in the assemblies tried to turn them into mini-parliaments, drawing extensively on English parliamentary tradition to justify their claims. One reason for the War for Independence was the failure

15

of the British government to appreciate the extent to which English constitutional principles had taken root in the colonies.

The English constitutional heritage emphasized the preservation of individual liberties against arbitrary power, and it had long suited the colonists to nourish this heritage. Repeatedly they insisted that they were Englishmen, entitled to all the rights and protections granted by the English constitution. If Englishmen at home were entitled, when accused of a criminal offence, to a trial by a jury of their peers, rather than by a judge sitting alone, then so were the subjects of the king in the American colonies, or so they believed. If men in England could not be taxed without their own consent, as given by their representatives in Parliament, the same applied to men in British America. When the members of the Continental Congress in 1774 remonstrated against the Coercive Acts they did so, they said, 'as Englishmen', and argued that their ancestors in emigrating had carried with them their full panoply of English rights, to which their colonial descendants were fully entitled.

The paradox of the American Revolution, then, is that it began in an assertion of the rights of free-born Englishmen. It is doubtful whether many of the first English settlers of the seventeenth century thought of themselves as carrying their full constitutional rights with them in their baggage. For one thing, as they were sailing the Atlantic the great constitutional battles of Stuart England were still being fought, and not until the Glorious Revolution of 1688–9 could the rights of Englishmen be defined with much confidence. As subjects themselves within the realm of the king, leading American colonists had an interest in the course of these constitutional struggles and were willing enough to profit from the victories of Parliamentarians and Whigs. For a variety of reasons, American conditions proved highly congenial to the more libertarian strands of English constitutional thought. In the political battles between Court and Country in eighteenth-century England the American colonists identified most readily with the Country position, with its distrust of central government and its sympathy for the House of Commons as the watch-dog of the people's liberties. Indeed, it was the more radical of Country critics to whom the American colonists warmed, the

Real Whigs or Commonwealthmen, who lamented the increasing influence of the executive over the legislature. The radicals did not have much effect in England, but their writings became popular in the American colonies.

Among these English radicals were John Trenchard and Thomas Gordon who, in the 1720s, published *Cato's Letters* in which they argued that England's celebrated constitution, which was supposed to preserve the liberties of Englishmen, was being subverted by the king's ministers who were using corruption to gain control over the other branches of government and establish a tyranny. A sinister and diabolical conspiracy, located in the Court, they said, was about to deprive Englishmen of their ancient liberties and impose on them a military despotism. These *Letters*, and others like them, were extensively circulated in the colonies. From *Cato's Letters* and from the writings of Lord Bolingbroke, James Burgh and other critics of British government, colonial and revolutionary Americans learned that in England the mixed constitution was being subverted by the machinations of the king and his ministers, who were allegedly wiping out the liberty of the people and the independence of the House of Commons by the use of bribery and patronage, and by the manipulation of the national debt and excise taxes. This image of a political order in which liberty was fast receding before the power of a voracious ministry immensely appealed to American colonists intent on protecting their own privileges. Further, as they became persuaded that liberty was dying out in England, they reached the ironical conclusion that they, the American colonists, were the last surviving champions of English rights.

This kind of mentality was sufficiently strong among influential Americans in the decade before 1775 to invest almost every imperial action with a sinister intent. Each successive measure of the British government seemed to fulfil the radical prophecy of a ministerial conspiracy to reduce America to servility. From this perspective, measures like the Stamp Act and the Townshend duties did seem like attempts to enslave them, to impose on them a form of government from which they were totally excluded.

This 'ideological' interpretation, one which rests on the world view of colonial leaders and their perceptions of British actions, goes a long way towards explaining American resistance. But ideology alone is not a sufficient explanation, partly because men do not live exclusively in the world of ideas, and partly because those with the greatest opportunity to immerse themselves in constitutional theory, the colonial gentry, were not the only men to rebel. The American resistance to British policy also owed something to economic considerations and to the interests, actions and beliefs of ordinary men and women.

Had the British measures confined themselves to empty declarations of the principle of parliamentary supremacy, as did the Declaratory Act, it is unlikely that the American colonists would have been provoked into open defiance. Empty gestures can be answered by empty gestures, as the Declaratory Act was. It was when influential colonists also felt themselves threatened economically by British policy that they were most sensitive to their constitutional rights and liberties. There are few things more effective than an unexpected tax demand for raising a man's political consciousness. This is not to suggest that the War for Independence was caused by the proposed taxes as such, only that they served to concentrate American minds on the political and constitutional status of the colonies within the British Empire.

The Seven Years War, or the French and Indian War as it was known in America, had generated a measure of prosperity, as wars often do, but the war was quickly followed by a depression which affected most of the colonies. The Sugar and Stamp Acts were passed by Parliament at a time when many American merchants were in severe distress, as were the shopkeepers and farmers who owed them money. Southern planters, too, found that the British demand for tobacco fell off, even as they were pressed to pay their debts to Britain merchants.

A flood of British imports forced some American merchants out of business and obliged others to stock their warehouses with goods they could not sell. The proposal to resist the Stamp Act by a boycott of British goods was thus welcomed by many merchants anxious to dispose of their own stocks at reasonable prices. Commercial conditions did thereafter improve, which is one reason why the colonists were slower to react to the Townshend duties of 1767, although non-importation did make headway in the northern ports as economic distress reappeared in places in the late 1760s. By the time that the Townshend duties were repealed in 1770 American merchants had disposed of their wares and were not prepared to maintain the boycott over the retention of the tea duty which, in any case, they could usually evade. But the return both of good times and of political peace was short-lived. The financial crisis which hit Britain in 1772, and which put the East India Company in such a precarious position, resulted in the collapse of credit in the colonies, the southern planters whose operations were dependent on Scottish and English credit being particularly affected. The merchants and planters who suffered these periodic crises continued to think of themselves as the loyal subjects of the English king, but they also on occasion attributed their economic difficulties to an imperial system over which they had no control. The British insistence that the colonies were subordinate to Parliament served only to deepen their anxieties.

If the colonial élites were conditioned by a libertarian ideology to interpret ministerial actions as evidence of an intent to enslave them, and if financial stringency periodically brought home to them their lack of economic independence, they were joined in their resistance to Britain by many Americans of lesser rank who had never read a political treatise or sought credit from a British merchant house. In part these artisans, tradesmen and small farmers participated in the intimidation of stamp distributors, customs officials and tea agents because they accepted the leadership of the gentry and were persuaded that their liberty too was threatened. As crowd action recurred in these years, however, new men of humble backgrounds emerged into positions of leadership, and some of them articulated a popular political ideology of their own. When Tom Paine, an eloquent and insubordinate Englishman of modest birth, arrived in Philadelphia in 1774, he quickly became a spokesman for the radical intellectuals and artisans of that city. His celebrated book, *Common Sense*, published in January 1776, went well beyond the traditional Country complaints about a corrupt executive subverting the liberty of the people, and denounced the English constitution itself, with its basis in monarchical and aristocratic 'tyranny'. Paine agreed that Americans were threatened with slavery, but the problem was not so much corruption as the hereditary principle. It was not only George III himself who was at fault but all kings. Such notions could be turned against hierarchies of any kind, and there were mechanics and small farmers who concluded that their own liberty would be secured only in a truly egalitarian society. These men supported the removal of royal authority as the first step to this democratic end.

Ideological considerations, then, moved some members of the lower orders, and their ideas were often more radical than those of the gentry. But they were also influenced by economic and personal interests. American seamen living in the colonial ports sometimes found themselves impressed into the Royal Navy, an experience which enabled them to link royal authority with tyranny; they had been denied both their livelihood and their liberty. Tradesmen and artisans in the city habitually bought on credit from local merchants during good times, and the financial crises which were roughly coincident with the Stamp Act and the Tea Act bankrupted these small men more quickly than they did their creditors. When American merchants in these years advocated the development of domestic manufacturing as a way of making their communities less dependent on Britain, members of the lower orders welcomed the employment opportunities that would be created. Many colonial craftsmen supported the boycotts of British goods arranged to combat the Stamp and Townshend duties because their own products would face less competition. As with the colonial gentry, economic interest often sharpened the perceptions of ordinary men that British policy could harm them, even reduce them to powerlessness or slavery.

Economic motives, then, help to explain the relatively early emergence of radicalism in the major American cities. But although the Sons of Liberty recruited members from all ranks in the cities, and helped to mobilize resistance to Britain, the significance of urban radicalism should not be exaggerated. The great majority of white men throughout the American colonies were small farmers, and they for the most part were not experiencing economic distress. The relative prosperity of agriculture was one reason why American farmers were slower to join the revolt against the king than urban tradesmen and mechanics, but they did eventually join and thus made possible the successful prosecution of the War for Independence. In the mid-1770s many of these farmers were drawn into the patriot cause by the persuasive advocacy of their betters, and many were politicized by the town and county meetings and committees which sprang up in these years, and by local churches and newspapers which perceived in British policy a threat to liberty. Literacy tended to be relatively high in the American countryside as well as in the cities, and newspapers and pamphlets left their mark.

In some areas, backcountry farmers were resentful towards those local gentlemen who had accepted office, land grants or other favours from the royal authorities, and were tempted to rebel to settle these local scores. Many small farmers throughout the colonies had been touched by the great religious awakening of the mid-eighteenth century, which had tended to turn them against the traditional ecclesiastical hierarchies. This egalitarian evangelicalism was still a powerful force at the time of the War for Independence, nurturing a suspicion of pomp, ostentation and hierarchy of all kinds. Some farmers took up arms against the king when they witnessed the depredations of his redcoats and hired mercenaries, and others when they calculated that their lives and land would best be protected through an association with the rebellion. A great many men in all the colonies were not initially strongly committed either to the patriot or the loyalist cause but, as the war turned against the British, increasing numbers saw the wisdom of declaring for the winning side. As with other social groups, those American farmers who rose in revolt did so for a variety of reasons, but without them independence could not have been achieved.

Whatever their personal motives, what ultimately united gentry and common men, city dwellers and farmers, was an agreement that British policy, whatever else it did, constituted a threat to American liberties. In the words of the Pennsylvanian leader, John Dickinson, '*Those* who are *taxed* without their own consent, expressed by themselves or their representatives, are *slaves*'. The measures of the British ministries after 1763, after all, were designed to secure greater imperial control over the colonies and were intended to raise some revenue from them, that is, to divert a little colonial property to defence and imperial purposes. In pamphlets, newspapers, legislative resolutions, speeches and sermons, Americans repeatedly used the term slavery to describe the condition to which they believed British policy was intended to consign them. Terminology of this sort was widely used throughout the English-speaking world in the eighteenth century, and the Country critics of the Whig administrations were quick enough to accuse the king's ministers of reducing Englishmen to slavery. But perhaps the term did carry an extra terror for the American colonists.

Chattel slavery, in the form of black slaves, existed in all thirteen colonies, although in much the greatest abundance in the plantation colonies of the south. When they spoke of Britain's intent to enslave America, the colonial leaders were speaking of political slavery; but the awful example of black slavery was not entirely absent from their consciousness. George Washington in 1774 complained that British measures could place white Americans in the same condition as black slaves. 'The crisis is arrived', he wrote, 'when we must assert our rights, or submit to every imposition, that can be heaped upon us, till custom and use shall make us tame and abject slaves, as the blacks we rule over with such arbitrary sway'.

Within each colony there were already human beings who were held in absolute bondage, men and women who had been born in slavery, reared in crippling ignorance, whose children would be slaves. There were husbands who had been separated from their wives, women who had been physically and sexually abused, children who had been sold away from their parents, labourers who had been exploited, beaten, mutilated and branded. When Americans spoke of the erosion of individual liberties as tending towards slavery, they had around them compelling evidence of what loss of freedom could mean. The existence of black slavery, perhaps, made white Americans more anxious to protect their own liberty. It is not entirely surprising that some of the most eloquent champions of American freedom were themselves slaveowners.

The irony of slaveowners emerging as upholders of liberty was not entirely lost on the revolutionary generation. 'With what consistency, or decency', asked Tom Paine in 1775, did the colonists 'complain so loudly of attempts to enslave them, while they hold so many hundred thousand in slavery'. The Continental Congress in April 1776, as it was remonstrating against the British incursions into American liberties, did in fact vote 'that no slaves be imported into any of the thirteen colonies'. Slavery and freedom had become curiously intertwined in America. On the one hand, as we have noted, black slavery served to make the white colonists more aware of the freedom that they themselves possessed and more inclined to scrutinize every British measure to see if it contained a threat to that freedom. In that sense the existence of black slavery may have contributed to the break with Britain, for it helped to turn white colonists into ardent libertarians, as far as their own rights were concerned. On the other hand, there was nothing to say that liberty was a monopoly of white men, and at least some champions of American rights realized the inconsistency of maintaining black slavery and began to look for ways of ending it. The Continental Congress did not and could not abolish slavery, but it made a tentative step in that direction with its call for the ending of the foreign slave trade. This, perhaps, enabled its members a few months later to vote for the Declaration of Independence with a clearer conscience. 'We hold these truths to be self-evident', said that remarkable document, 'that all men are created equal, that they are endowed by their Creator with certain unalienable Rights, that among these are Life, Liberty and the pursuit of Happiness'. It was a slaveowner who had composed those words, but forever after Americans could use them against any form of slavery or subjection.

The War for Independence

Hostilities had broken out over a year before the adoption of the Declaration of Independence. When the Continental Congress met in May 1775, soon after the Battle of Lexington, many of its members still hoped that the differences between London and the colonies might be resolved and that Americans might remain loyal subjects of the king. In July, indeed, Congress adopted the 'Olive Branch Petition', professing loyalty to the king and asking him to use his influence to avert hostilities. But it was not too late for re-conciliation. After the skirmish at Lexington on 19 April the British troops had moved on to Concord, where they exchanged fire with the Massachusetts militia and destroyed the powder and arms the colonists had been collecting there. They then returned to Boston, which colonial forces proceeded to besiege. News of these confrontations flashed around the colonies, and extra-legal assemblies, town meetings and local militia bands readied themselves for war. Close to the Canadian border a group of Vermonters led by Ethan Allen took possession of Fort Ticonderoga on Lake Champlain in May. A few weeks later, on 17 June 1775, when General Gage tried to secure the defence of Boston, he won a technical victory at the Battle of Bunker Hill, but at the cost of over a thousand British casualties, more than twice the American losses. This was the bloodiest engagement of the entire war, which could not now be stopped. Congress had already decided to raise a Continental Army and had appointed George Washington as commander-in-chief. In July Congress adopted a Declaration of Causes of Taking Up Arms, which still claimed a desire for reconciliation but which made clear that Americans would 'dye Free-men rather than live Slaves'.

MAJOR BATTLES OF THE WAR FOR INDEPENDENCE

A. PRE-INDEPENDENCE ENGAGEMENTS

April 1775	Battles of Lexington and Concord (Massachusetts)
May 1775	Fort Ticonderoga (New York) taken by Americans
June 1775	Battle of Bunker Hill (Massachusetts)
March 1776	Boston (Massachusetts) abandoned by British

Declaration of Independence, 4 July 1776

B. THE WAR IN THE NORTH

August 1776	Battle of Long Island (New York)
September 1776	New York City taken by British
December 1776	Battle of Trenton (New Jersey)
January 1777	Battle of Princeton (New Jersey)

possessing over three times the population of the United States, a professional army and navy, and infinitely greater financial resources. George III and his ministers, like most people in Britain, understandably assumed that British victory was certain, which was one reason why they were prepared to resort to military measures. Yet within two years Britain was losing the war and in 1781 the surrender of General Cornwallis at Yorktown marked the final humiliation of British might. The infant United States, against the apparent odds, had emerged victorious. It would be more accurate to say, however, not that the United States won the war but that Britain lost it. She did so in part for strategic and logistical reasons. A war could not easily be fought across three thousand miles of ocean and many thousands of square miles of unfriendly terrain. Further, the British suffered because of important miscalculations, in particular in overestimating the degree of potential loyalist support in America. Finally, the entry of France into the war and Britain's need to protect herself elsewhere in the world denied her the opportunity of focusing exclusively on defeating the American rebels. Britain's generals did not acquit themselves as badly as has sometimes been alleged but they were fighting a war that they could not win.

In the early years, in particular, the British underestimated the extent of resistance and counted on most Americans to stay loyal. The Coercive Acts and the appointment of Thomas Gage as the military governor of Massachusetts in 1774 had been based on the assumption that Boston was the hub of discontent and that the American problem would be solved by detaching and subduing this tiresome area. Yet the engagements of Lexington, Concord and Bunker Hill served to arouse the rebellious ardour of Americans throughout the colonies, and suggested that the British were not invulnerable. Thomas Gage was replaced by Sir William Howe as the British commander in Massachusetts, but as his troops sat around in beseiged Boston the British hoped for some support from the south. Loyalism was said to be strong in North and South Carolina, and a British army was despatched from Ireland with the object of joining up with loyalist troops in North Carolina. The loyalist support failed to materialize, however, and the British force under Sir Henry Clinton sailed on towards New

York. Meanwhile, Sir William Howe had concluded that Boston could not be defended and in March 1776 he left with his men for Halifax, Nova Scotia. At the beginning of July 1776, with Howe abandoning Boston and Clinton abandoning the south, there was no British army left in the thirteen colonies. The plan of ending the rebellion by isolating it in Massachusetts had failed. American resistance was more widespread than the ministry had realized and loyalist support unreliable.

With the quitting of Boston, British planning entered a second and more conventional phase, that of seeking to engage and defeat American troops in battle. Military success, the British believed, would make possible the resumption of British political rule. This too was a miscalculation, for isolated military victories did little to win the hearts of Americans for the king. Nevertheless, Howe decided that the key was New York City, a loyalist stronghold. If this could be taken New England would be cut off from the south and might be subdued by military action. In July British troops again set foot on American soil, and after defeating George Washington at the Battle of Long Island in August they captured New York, which they held for the rest of the war. Engagements followed in neighbouring New Jersey, and Washington was forced across the Delaware river into Pennsylvania. But the British lines were now spread thin, and on Christmas night Washington returned across the Delaware and captured a thousand Hessian mercenaries at Trenton. (The British government had been obliged to hire these German soldiers because of the shortage of British troops, who were scattered in many posts around the empire.) Washington followed his success at Trenton with a victory over the British at Princeton in January 1777.

By the beginning of 1777, then, General Howe, a slow and cautious man, had failed to secure much advantage from his hold on New York City. Indeed, the recent American victories had raised the patriots' morale. But the British believed that in 1777 events would turn decisively their way. As well as Howe's army in New York, the British had a large army in Canada, and if the two could be joined up the New England states could be cut off from the others. A plan was devised which was to require General

John Burgoyne to take a Canadian army down Lake Champlain southwards towards Albany, while another force was to head eastwards for Albany from Lake Ontario. British troops would thus occupy the Hudson Valley and be in a position to reinforce General Howe in New York City. As this operation to supply Howe with troops from Canada was being mounted, Howe decided to use the summer of 1777 to try to take Philadelphia by sea. This he succeeded in doing by the end of September, and in the process he inflicted some minor defeats on George Washington but, more importantly, he failed to destroy Washington's army, which settled down for a desolate winter at Valley Forge. Washington's cold, hungry and ragged soldiers suffered badly that winter, but they survived.

In the meantime, the plan to bring the large British army south from Canada was going badly astray. It did take Fort Ticonderoga, but as it advanced the rebels destroyed bridges, blocked roads and harassed its flanks. More seriously, the projected reinforcements from Lake Ontario failed to get through, leaving General Burgoyne's army exposed and its supply line from Canada dangerously extended. Burgoyne had in fact attempted to bring ample supplies with him, including thirty carts of champagne and other comforts for his own personal use, but the roads were barely passable, the horses too few and breakdowns too many.

The clumsy British invasion also goaded many otherwise peaceable farmers into armed defiance. When a British force attempted to starve out a rebel garrison at Fort Schuyler, local German settlers rose in revolt. When a girl was killed and scalped by Indians who were fighting for the British, and when Burgoyne seemed to threaten further Indian atrocities, more indignant Americans joined the rebel cause. In the event Burgoyne's southward advance towards Albany was blocked by American forces commanded by General Gates, while New England militia menaced his flanks from the east. Desertions and reduced rations further demoralized the stalled British army, which was now confronted by almost four times as many American troops. Eventually General Burgoyne found himself surrounded, and in October 1777 he surrendered at Saratoga. The year in which the

British had expected to win the war turned out to be the year in which they effectively lost it. Washington's army was still largely intact while Britain's important Canadian army was no more. The British had suffered a major and humiliating defeat and had little to show for their campaigns apart from General Howe's rather pointless occupation of Philadelphia.

Saratoga changed the course of the war decisively in favour of the United States. One major consequence was French recognition of the United States and French entry into the war in 1778 as an American ally. In 1779 Spain also entered the war against Britain. In the following year British resources were strained yet further by the League of Armed Neutrality, organized by Russia, Sweden and Denmark to protect neutral trade, and by Holland, which also joined the war. Britain now found almost the whole of Europe arrayed against her. She was no longer in undisputed control of the sea, and her loss of supremacy in American waters in particular was seriously to injure her war effort.

After Saratoga the war entered a third phase, as Britain recognized that military engagements alone would not bring victory. Quite apart from the distractions presented by the European belligerents, the British recognized that it was necessary to win over the civilian population. The focus of the war shifted to the south, where the British still believed loyalism to be strong. In any case, the entry of France into the war meant that Britain was obliged to divert some troops to the West Indies, with the result that the Americans regained Philadelphia and Rhode Island. Restricted to their New York stronghold in the north, the British now hoped to use their navy and the reputed presence of loyalists to pacify the South Carolina–Georgia area. In 1778–9 the British largely won control of Georgia. In 1780 Sir Henry Clinton captured Charleston and took 5000 American prisoners, while Lord Cornwallis defeated an American army at Camden, leaving the British in possession of South Carolina. With the South Carolina–Georgia region under control, the British under Lord Cornwallis attempted to carry their supremacy into North Carolina, but here they met reverses. At the Battle of Cowpens in January 1781 British troops were defeated by General Daniel Morgan. The British also suffered serious losses, although they claimed a technical victory, at Guilford Court House, where they were taken by surprise by General Nathanael Greene. Further, as the British army moved north patriots reclaimed the southern countryside. Unable to inflict a decisive defeat on the American forces, and discouraged by the failure of loyalists to materialize in any substantial way, Cornwallis withdrew to Wilmington on the coast. The American forces reasserted their hold in the interior, confining the British troops under Cornwallis to the North Carolina coastline. The British attempt to win over the south with loyalist aid had failed by the spring of 1781.

Cornwallis saw little advantage in lingering in the Carolinas, and in April 1781 he abandoned the area, pressing northward into Virginia, where there were still some British troops. He marched his men to Yorktown, on Chesapeake Bay, with the intention of constructing a naval base there. If the king's army could be supplied by the Royal Navy it would be invincible, capable of being directed against almost any accessible American target. The success of this strategy, however, depended on the British control of Chesapeake Bay, and in fact it was a French fleet which arrived there first. When British ships reached Chesapeake from New York they proved incapable of expelling the French. Meanwhile George Washington, who had been apprised of French intentions, marched his army south to Virginia, and Lord Cornwallis found himself cornered at Yorktown. Washington was able to lay siege with over twice as many troops as were in the British command. Cornwallis was short of ammunition and ill equipped for a long siege: on 19 October 1781 he surrendered. The importance to the Americans of the French alliance was vividly illustrated by this affair. Not only had the French fleet made it impossible for Cornwallis to escape by sea, but nearly half of the troops at Washington's disposal were French. The mortifying British surrender at Yorktown effectively marked the end of hostilities in North America.

For a second time since the war began a major British army had been forced to surrender. The American war was proving a long, expensive and futile one for the British government, which now realized that it had little alternative but to abandon the attempt to coerce her former colonies. British trade had been seriously injured by the war, British forces were suffering reverses at the hands of the European powers elsewhere in the world, and the British were encountering severe difficulties in governing Ireland and India. In February 1783 the House of Commons resolved to end military measures against the Americans, much to the disappointment of the king. In March Lord North resigned and was succeeded by ministers eager to make peace with the rebels. The grieving king briefly contemplated abdication, but eventually agreed to send a representative to Paris to open peace negotiations.

Making peace proved a difficult process, but eventually the Treaty of Paris was signed in September 1783 and it recognized American independence. The American negotiators, Benjamin Franklin, John Jay and John Adams, however, achieved a great deal more than that. They also secured for the new nation much of the American interior, the land between the Alleghenies and the Mississippi, and recogniton of traditional American fishing rights off Newfoundland. The Americans, for their part, agreed to 'recommend' to the states that the property confiscated from the loyalists be returned to them. In November 1783 the last British troops set sail from New York. The fledgling United States of America had bested one of the world's great powers.

American success in the War for Independence owed something to the competence and good sense of generals like George Washington and Nathanael Greene, who proved themselves a match for their more experienced British counterparts. But, ultimately, it was British failure more than American military prowess which determined the outcome of the war. Strategically and logistically the British were at a considerable disadvantage. Keeping troops supplied across three thousand miles of water and more of land was no easy task, and while George Washington's army at times suffered fearful deprivations, the king's soldiers were repeatedly poorly transported, fed and housed. American territory was vast and unfamiliar, its inhabitants for the most part unfriendly. The British also tended to cling to outdated military ideas and methods. If the United States lacked an experienced army, Americans were well versed in the use of firearms, particularly the American rifle, which was superior to the British smoothbore musket, and they proved more skilled at the guerrilla warfare which developed. More seriously, perhaps, the British made a number of fatal miscalculations, as in their initial belief that the rebellion was more localized than it proved to be, and in their assumption that winning conventional battles would win the war. Similarly they frequently over estimated the degree of loyalist support which they could expect. In the end, however, the soldiers of the king simply could not subdue a continent. They could take important towns like New York and Philadelphia, and they could win pitched battles like that of Camden, but such victories brought the British little advantage when the population remained hostile. Whenever the redcoats moved out of a particular area it reverted to the patriot cause. There were military mistakes, too, as when Burgoyne at Saratoga and Cornwallis at Yorktown led their armies into positions which were beyond the reach of supplies or reinforcements, and from which there was no escape. And finally the entry of France into the war swung the struggle decisively in America's favour. Britain was thereafter fighting on several fronts, her forces were dispersed, and the French were able to provide the Americans with crucial assistance at sea. George Washington and his fellow generals were never able to clear their country of British troops and they never established military dominance. In that sense they could not claim to have won the war. But they did not abandon the struggle while the British eventually did.

The revolutions within the states

While the patriots were fighting the redcoats they were also coming to realize that they were, after all, conducting a revolution. The war itself may not have been a revolution, and it may have started as an attempt to preserve English liberties from the usurpations of British ministers, but once it had begun it accelerated the pace of revolutionary change within America. Colonials who had initially resisted British impositions by citing their rights 'as Englishmen' were soon speaking of the natural rights of men everywhere and were emphatically denying that they were Englishmen. As patriotism encouraged them to seek a new character, they also began to consider what political institutions would be appropriate for a republic. The removal of royal authority meant that the several states had hastily to construct new governments, and these were inevitably shaped in part by the popular and democratic currents unleashed by the War for Independence. The thirteen colonies had been separate entities, and the new states naturally enough retained their distinctive identities. The revolutionary movement within America in the years immediately after the Declaration of Independence cannot easily be thought of as a national movement. Rather, it was in the local communities and the separate states that this phase of the revolution unfolded.

The Declaration of Independence pronounced the former colonies to be 'Free and Independent States', but it said nothing about their forms of government. That was a matter for them. None the less, in rejecting the rule of George III it was obvious that the United States was to be a republic – or perhaps thirteen republics. Republicanism, however, implied a good deal more than the simple absence of a monarch. Tom Paine defined the word republic as 'the *public* good, or the good of the whole', arguing that there should be no 'interest distinct from that of the nation'. Rule by nobility, oligarchy or faction was no more compatible with republicanism than rule by a king. The idea of republicanism was not as yet interchangeable with the idea of democracy, but it did imply a form of government which represented the whole people and only the people.

In many ways America was well suited to republicanism, even before the Declaration of Independence. In the colonial period there had been no king, lords or bishops personally present. All colonists were commoners, members of the third estate, and the social élites which had emerged, however wealthy, had been of low-born derivation. No American could claim to be born to rule. The absence of a distinct ruling class meant that there was no realistic alternative to some form of popular government, once the break with England occurred. Further, property was relatively widely distributed in the colonies. The availability of land meant that most white men held some property, and as such could claim a stake and hence a voice in society. Since it was property which conferred the suffrage in the colonial period, the majority of white men held the right to vote. The 'political nation' of 1750 was proportionately far more extensive in the colonies than in England. Further, these small property holders were for the most part represented in the legislatures, whereas in England even many members of the middle class were not directly represented in Parliament. In several colonies, as pointed out earlier, substantial power had come to rest with the legislatures well before 1776. In the eyes of some Englishmen, even before the War for Independence, the American colonies were already practising forms of republicanism.

If colonial society and politics sometimes seemed to visiting Englishmen to be uncomfortably democratic, they became even more so with the collapse of British rule. As the gentry passed ringing resolutions against British tyranny in the colonial and provincial assemblies, men of lesser rank took to the streets to intimidate stamp distributors, royal officials and loyalists and, once fighting had broken out, enrolled in the local militias and the Continental Army. The Sons of Liberty which emerged in the cities in the mid-1760s contained many artisans, tradesmen and small merchants, and they helped to raise the political consciousness of Americans generally, drawing many ordinary citizens into the fight against Britain. As committees of correspondence, county meetings and popular conventions spread across the land to co-ordinate American resistance, they often took over the functions of local government. In the two years before the Declaration of Independence judges and magistrates appointed by the royal authorities sometimes found themselves ignored by local committees and crowds which took the law into their own hands. These local communities were conducting revolutions of their own, for authority was now coming from below rather than above. Critical community decisions continued to be made by popularly chosen committees during the war itself, particularly in its early years.

These committees brought many new men into politics and turned some of them into radical democrats. Their influence was not confined to the local level. State governments also had to be created, and while some of these continued to be dominated by the same social élites which had filled the old colonial assemblies, others contained men of lesser rank. Far-reaching political and social changes were thus taking place in America, but the degree of change varied from state to state. The new state constitutions which were drawn up in these years themselves reflected the range of political opinions held by Americans.

In South Carolina and Maryland, for example, where wealthy planters had long wielded considerable political influence, the constitutions sought to limit popular participation by such devices as high property qualifications for office, and ensured that the conservative eastern regions, with their large property-owners, were well represented in the legislatures. As in England, political rights were still very much attached to property, and curbs were placed on democracy.

In Pennsylvania and Georgia, on the other hand, highly democratic constitutions were adopted, with taxpaying or very modest property qualifications allowing almost all white men to vote, and with sheriffs and other officials being elected locally. This meant that local communities would continue largely to govern their own affairs. These two states underlined their commitment to democracy by deciding to have a legislature consisting of a single house – there would be no senate or upper chamber in which an aristocracy might entrench itself.

Several states tried to balance the contending interests of property and democracy in their constitutions. Massachusetts and New York, for example, divided their legislatures into two, and ensured that property-owners were well represented in the upper houses or senates while in the lower houses seats were apportioned roughly according to the distribution of population. The representation of property in one house would thus be offset by the representation of people in the other. These arrangements were hardly models of democracy, but the popular currents awakened by the confrontation with royal authority had clearly left their mark. Having proclaimed the principle of 'no taxation without representation' in their quarrels with Britain, the American rebels had to see that the people were well represented in their own forms of government. The suffrage was already extensive in America by English standards, but in these years about half of the states widened it further, so that perhaps three-quarters of white men held the right to vote, and more in some states.

One way in which these constitutions leaned in the direction of the people was in their emphasis on the legislative branch of government. Their long quarrels with the royal authorities had convinced Americans that the main threat to liberty was a power-hungry executive, and so the role of the executive was greatly reduced. Each state government was formally headed by a governor, except for Pennsylvania which managed to do without one, but the governors were little more than figureheads, most of them being denied even the power to veto laws. It was the legislatures which ruled, particularly the lower houses, which were normally elected annually. The men who determined government policy were thus obliged to present themselves to their electoral masters at frequent intervals – and so a crippling restraint was placed even on legislative power. The Americans had learned from the English radicals that 'where annual election ends, tyranny begins', and sought to avert any possibility of enslavement by placing government essentially in the hands of bodies elected each year by the people. If, under the old system, power had seemed to reside mainly in a distant executive, now it was to reside mainly in a popularly elected and relatively accessible legislature.

When these legislatures met they were found to be composed of men 'not quite so well dressed, not so politely educated, nor so highly born as some Assemblies I have formerly seen', according to one observant Virginian. Men from the well-to-do classes usually remained influential in the state legislatures, but the proportion of small farmers and others of moderate means did rise dramatically in several of them. One reason for this was the enlargement of the legislatures themselves and the better representation in them of western and other districts whose claims had been previously neglected. According to the estimates of Jackson Turner Main, overall the proportion of large landowners, lawyers and merchants declined from something like 60 per cent in the recent colonial assemblies to around 35 per cent in the new state legislatures, while the proportion of small farmers and artisans roughly doubled from 20 to 40 per cent. The long-powerful élite groups which represented landed, commercial, urban and creditor interests were now often confronted in the legislatures by loose political groupings speaking up for small farmer, artisan, rural and debtor interests. The gentry had not altogether lost power, but they were obliged to share it, and their authority was now regularly questioned by men of more humble rank.

In the sense that there was a substantial redistribution of power and authority, there were revolutionary movements in America, but the revolutions were being conducted at local and state levels. There was, it could almost be said, a Pennsylvanian revolution and a Georgian revolution, but not as yet an American revolution, if by that is implied a national phenomenon. The American struggle with Britain, and the Commonwealth tradition itself, had bred a distrust of central authority, and for the most part the Americans were reluctant to place much power in a national government. The Continental Congress did frame a national constitutional structure, the Articles of Confederation, which eventually came into effect in 1781. The Articles allowed each state to retain its prized individual sovereignty, while certain functions were delegated to a Congress, consisting of a single house in which each state had one vote. There was no national executive and even the Congress was not allowed to exercise much authority. It could not regulate trade or levy taxes and at times it barely functioned at all, for the state governments frequently ignored it and even its own members often found better things to do than attend its sessions. The United States remained a loose collection of individual states, without much in the way of a national society or government. There was nothing necessarily wrong in this, at least in the view of many. Whatever the deficiencies of Congress, it had, after all, successfully waged a war and concluded an advantageous peace treaty with one of the world's most powerful nations. The ending of the war made a national government seem less imperative, and many Americans continued to dislike the idea of a central authority which might resist the democratization of state and local politics. Besides, if Americans no longer thought of themselves as Englishmen, they still thought of themselves as Virginians or New Yorkers first and Americans second.

At the heart of the movement for independence had been the

question of individual liberties – whether a government could direct or tax a man without his consent – and the American revolutionaries continued to address themselves to this question in their several states. As noted above, the state governments generally were so arranged that most settled areas were represented in them and so that the great majority of taxpayers possessed the vote. Most states also adopted declarations of rights, recognizing such individual liberties as freedom of worship, trial by jury, and protection against cruel and unusual punishments. This libertarian impulse in itself sometimes required that distinct breaks be made with the past. Established churches, for example, had existed in most of the colonies, and revolutionary Americans now had to consider whether a religious establishment was consistent with individual liberties. In fact the Congregational churches, which had joined the revolt against England, did survive as established churches in Massachusetts and Connecticut, but in Virginia Thomas Jefferson's Bill for Establishing Religious Freedom, adopted in 1785, set a precedent for the future when it severed all connection between church and state. No church was to enjoy privileges denied to others and no man was to suffer any formal disadvantages because of his religion. If all men were created equal, as Jefferson wrote in the Declaration of Independence, that equality was to extend to his private beliefs as well as to his public rights.

The libertarian ideas on which the revolution was based also called into question the position of black slavery. As one American clergyman pointed out to his fellow rebels in 1776, black Americans have 'as good a right to liberty as ourselves'. Most white men were uncomfortable with this line of argument, even in the northern states, but some of them conceded that the revolutionary commitment to the inalienable rights of man should mean an ending to chattel slavery. Some slaves had actually fought against the crown in the War for Independence, and these for the most part were given their freedom at the end of their army service. Anti-slavery societies first appeared in these years, and individual owners began to take it upon themselves to free their slaves. This was easiest in the northern states, where there were relatively few slaves, and in 1780 Pennsylvania provided for the gradual abolition of slavery. Other northern states, too, moved to adopt gradual emancipation schemes, although in some it took decades for slavery to disappear. Where emancipation occurred, however, it did not mean equality, for even the most ardent of white libertarians found it difficult to throw off the accumulated prejudices of the past. Blacks were sometimes accorded a status similar to Indians, not slaves but hardly citizens either, for their civil and political rights were restricted and uncertain. The great majority of slaves, in any case, lived in the Atlantic states of the south, and there they were too important to the plantation economy, and too numerous, for those societies seriously to consider emancipation. Southern slave masters, when confronted with the question of whether black slavery was consistent with the revolutionary claim that all men were created equal, eventually tried to persuade themselves and others that blacks were not after all entitled to equal rights, that they were different from white men and indeed inferior. If the example of slavery had once encouraged white Americans to proclaim their own liberties, the libertarian ideology of the revolutionary era in turn intensified racist assumptions in the south.

The success of anti-slavery measures in some northern states and the strengthening of pro-slavery sentiments in the southern states illustrate the varying courses that the revolutionary movement took in different parts of the country. In the 1770s and 1780s the several societies which had once constituted British America were shaken to their foundation. Countless distinguished and anonymous citizens, in their town, county and state communities, together conducted their own political revolutions, if not social revolutions, winning a measure of control over the societies in which they lived. The degree of revolutionary change varied from state to state, and no state carried the revolution to a truly radical conclusion. There were loyalists who continued to sympathize with the king, but while they often lost their lands and were sometimes obliged to flee, none of them lost their heads as did luckless aristocrats in France a few years later. Apart from the confiscation of loyalist estates, there were no serious attempts to redistribute property or wealth within the state societies in these years. Rich patriots retained their wealth, and often their influence. None of the new state constitutions gave the vote to all men regardless of other qualifications, not even to all white men, and in most of them property-owners retained some privileges. The revolutionary upheavals, then, did not level these American societies. But they did profoundly change them. Large numbers of ordinary men were drawn into politics, power was no longer monopolized by the gentry, the people were more fully represented in the new constitutions, and the state governments became highly responsive to popular opinion. In most states a political revolution had been accomplished, one that could not easily be undone, even if it did little to create a new nation.

The revolution in the nation

The uneven, unpredictable, but often far-reaching redistribution of political authority in the local communities and states which together made up the United States was taking place in the same years as the War for Independence. By 1783 a revolution had been conducted, but not an *American* revolution, if by that is meant a *national* occurrence. The inhabitants of the United States, after all, never had been one people, certainly not in the days of British rule, and while the cause of independence forced the sovereign states to attempt to work together, it also released a host of pressures which set different groups of Americans spinning away from one another. The 'Green Mountain Boys' in the hinterland of New York and New Hampshire, for example, decided that they did not like New York's relatively conservative constitution and broke away to form a state of their own, Vermont. In many ways the shifting and variegated social and political order of the United States functioned well enough. Law and order generally prevailed, American citizens were for the most part fed, housed and clothed, and their governments were more responsive to their demands than ever before. And yet there were Americans, particulary among the gentry, who were disappointed with what they saw around them as the war with Britain ended. States and communites had been shaken up, but there was little awareness in them of their being part of a *national* society. For many of those members of the gentry who had served during the war in national offices rather than in state offices, perhaps in the Continental

Army, or in Congress, or as ministers abroad, this was a cause for grief. They had developed a grander vision of their nation's destiny, and in the 1780s they turned to the task of making the revolution a truly national phenomenon.

For men like George Washington and John Adams a kind of national revolution had taken place, as the struggle for independence created a national consciousness among the leadership. But if George Washington began to think of himself as an American first and a Virginian second, most ordinary people continued to identify with their local communities and at most with their state governments. By the mid-1780s the revolutionary gentry were realizing, to their horror, that their own revolution had not extended down to the people, that the volatile state governments were still going their own way with little regard for the national reputation of the United States.

Superficially, the gentry had grounds for complaint. States often did put their own interests first, such as by imposing higher tariffs than others against foreign goods. Individual states made their own wars and treaties with Indian tribes, though this was meant to be a federal responsibility. Different naturalization laws obtained in the different states, so that alien immigrants might evade the stringent regulations of one state by acquiring citizenship in another, which entitled them to citizenship rights in any state. Some members of the gentry complained of the irresponsible legislation of some states, such as laws designed to ease the problems of debtors through substituting paper money for hard coin. In Rhode Island, for example, rioting broke out when the legislature tried to make creditors accept payment for debts in depreciating paper currency. Those gentlemen who wanted the United States to assume a dignified stance in the world were also worried by the powerlessness of the national government. Its deficit increased every year, and attempts to give Congress a revenue through an impost on imports failed, because it was never possible to secure the necessary consent of all the states. Meanwhile, Congress found that it could not even pay the interest on the wartime debts it had contracted with American citizens and with France. Nor could it impose its will on foreign powers which treated the United States with disrespect. British troops continued to occupy forts in the north-west, despite the Treaty of Paris, and Spain, which had regained Florida and the Gulf Coast, handicapped western settlers by closing the mouth of the Mississippi to American commerce. Alexander Hamilton expressed the views of the revolutionary gentry when he wrote in 1782: 'There is something . . . contemptible in the prospect of a number of petty states, . . . fluctuating and unhappy at home, weak and insignificant by their dissentions in the eyes of other nations.'

This view, that the United States was falling apart, was not shared by most Americans, however. The wayward behaviour of the state governments offended the national vision and ambitions of the more worldly gentry, but ordinary people generally continued to make their living without any sense of impending anarchy. In many ways government under the Articles of Confederation acquitted itself well. Several of the problems of the 1780s, after all, would have existed whatever the system of government. There was a brief economic depression following the departure of the British troops, but American farmers and merchants were soon prospering again and manufactures were being established. Congress may not have been able to pay its debts, but a number of states began to assume responsibility for the debts owed to their own citizens. The problem of repaying foreign loans was a more difficult, though not necessarily insuperable one. The national government, after all, had a potential source of revenue in the vast territory to the west, the disposal (and selling off) of which was in the hands of Congress. British troops might be lingering in the frontier forts, but the United States had already demonstrated her ability to beat Britain, and no one seriously expected a military attack from Britain or any other foreign power. Spain might be disrupting American commerce in the Mississippi, but in principle that was a dispute that could be resolved by negotiation. Some of the laws passed by individual states were no doubt unwise, but they were rarely oppressive, and most state governments muddled along competently enough by eighteenth-century standards. There was no overwhelming economic or military reason for abandoning the Articles of Confederation, and in theory the United States could have developed as a league of sovereign states, rather like the modern European Community.

The revolutionary gentry, however, disdained such a mundane and disorderly future. They wanted a unified republic which would span a continent (or at least a large part of it), and which would command the respect of the world. They wanted to create a truly national society in which the distinctions between New Yorkers, Marylanders and Virginians would be no more, in which local and state attachments were subordinate to national loyalties. Having developed a national consciousness themselves during their leadership of the war, their own pride and prestige became identified with those of the nation. But it was not only patriotism which led them to deplore the localist and centrifugal pressures which they discerned all around them. As men of high status they were cool towards the popular and democratic tendencies in state and local government. An excess of local democracy, they sensed, would both frustrate their national objectives and imperil their own positions. In one sense their desire to reconstruct the national government was counter-revolutionary, for a high-toned government at the centre might counteract democracy in the states. But they were not crude reactionaries, and they recognized that government at any level in the United States had to be seen to represent the people. America's popular revolution might be channelled in new and steadier directions, but it had gone too far to be suppressed.

In the years after the British surrender at Yorktown, America's nationalistic gentlemen were looking for ways of strengthening the central government. They magnified every imperfection in the Articles of Confederation and they pointed to the constant changes in state laws as evidence of the instability of state government. Their fears that the republic was dissolving into anarchy seemed vindicated by Shays' Rebellion in 1786, when the hard-pressed farmers of western Massachusetts rose in rebellion against the courts which were trying to enforce the collection of debts and taxes. The rising was soon dispersed, but alarmed and highly placed citizens across the nation redoubled their efforts to hold a convention in Philadelphia to amend the constitution. Several state legislatures were persuaded to send delegates to the

43

convention, which duly met in the summer of 1787, and which instead of amending the old constitution wrote a new one. A new constitution, the gentry hoped, would communicate their own vision of a national society to the people at large. As gentlemen, they took it for granted that stable societies were hierarchical in form, and through what became known as the American Constitution they offered a new hierarchy to direct the nation's affairs.

By 1789 a constitutional revolution, though not a social revolution, had been completed in the United States on a national scale. While the American Constitution did introduce a new hierarchy, it none the less broke with English precedent by establishing a national system of government which was wholly elective, apart from the judiciary. Never had a government existed in a populous nation in which all the branches stemmed from the people and only the people. America's gentry were certainly anxious to counter the unreliable state governments with an imposing national edifice, but they knew that their new Constitution would only be accepted by Americans generally if it recognized the need for popular participation. Hence the Constitution was designed to reconcile hierarchy with democracy. The key to this was the principle of representation. Ideally, the people would elect their betters to represent them.

The national government envisaged by the Constitution was to be stronger than before. There was to be a Congress with certain specified powers, including the right to impose taxes and to provide for the national defence. It was to be divided into a Senate, with the authority to ratify treaties and presidential appointments, and a House of Representatives, which was to initiate money bills. A separate executive was created, for the first time at the national level, headed by a President who possessed the right to veto legislation, enjoyed substantial powers to execute the law, and was also commander-in-chief. In addition to the legislature and the executive, a separate national judiciary, headed by a Supreme Court, whose members were to be appointed by the President and confirmed by the Senate, would have an oversight of the laws. This national government would clearly be possessed of some authority, and its hierarchical nature was underlined by the arrangements for electing its different branches.

44

The House of Representatives, whose members were to be distributed among the different states according to the sizes of their populations, was to be elected every two years directly by the voters in each state. The Senate was to consist of two Senators from each state, chosen by the state legislators. This indirect method of election, it was hoped, would ensure that Senators would be men of some stature, and, befitting their superior wisdom, they would serve for six years. The President, with a four-year term, was also to be elected indirectly, by an electoral college chosen specially for the purpose. Each state was to have as many presidential electors as it had members in Congress, and these electors were to be chosen as the state legislature directed, perhaps by popular vote or perhaps by the legislature itself. Such a system of election, Alexander Hamilton argued, would weed out unsuitable candidates and increase the chances of the presidency being filled 'by characters pre-eminent for ability and virtue'. Further, the constituencies which these new national officers represented, even members of Congress, were very large when compared to those that most state politicians represented, which should put men of prominence at an advantage in any electoral competition. In these ways, the nation's gentlemen hoped that national office would fall on themselves, so that they could use their new authority to impress on their fellow citizens the need to put nation before state.

Yet the framers of the Constitution also saw that a revolution had largely transformed state and local politics and that an unpopular Constitution could not be forced on the people. Any new hierarchy could only come into being with popular consent, and this was sought in a number of ways. The indirect systems of election for President and Senate may have been designed to elevate the better sort, but the bodies which chose them were themselves ultimately elected by the people, that is by the qualified voters. (The Constitution left it to each state to determine its own suffrage.) In this sense, all the officers of government, however mighty, were to be the agents of the people, in a way that no king of England could ever be. The framers of the Constitution remained true to the representative principle at almost every point. Further, the people were to be asked to ratify the Constitution. The framers requested each state to hold a convention 'expressly chosen by the people' to accept or reject the Constitution, which was to come into effect after nine states had agreed to it. Never before in history had a people been in a position expressly to consent to the national institutions by which they were to be governed. This was a remarkable though probably unavoidable compliance with the principle of popular sovereignty. At this point the battle was joined, for there were those who saw the Constitution as an authoritarian device. Across the country nationally minded gentlemen, with the support of many urban artisans and of commercial farmers too, became known as Federalists as they fought for the Constitution, while locally minded gentlemen and many rural citizens and backwoods farmers contributed to the Anti-Federalist resistance to the Constitution. After the Federalists had conceded a bill of rights, to protect individual and state liberties, they won the day. They could claim that the people had consented to a new hierarchy to govern them.

The national gentry had carried through a constitutional revolution, creating a sound national government which took its authority from below. Through this medium they hoped to effect a political revolution, conveying their own national consciousness down to the people, who might now be pulled into an involvement with national affairs. Only then, in the eyes of many of the gentry, would a truly American Revolution have been accomplished. But in the end they failed to produce such a revolution. The world of most Americans continued to stop at their town, county or state boundaries. The Constitution was indeed ratified in popularly elected state conventions, but only about one-fifth of the white men in the country turned out to vote in those elections (and some of them voted for Anti-Federalist candidates). A new national government did come into existence in 1789, but most Americans continued to ignore that government. America's gentlemen did establish themselves in Congress and (when it was built) in the White House, but most of the nation's qualified voters stayed at home on election days. For many years voter turnout in state elections, such as for the governor, was higher than the turnout in presidential elections.

Americans across the land elected town councils and state governments and expected them to maintain law and order, to resolve land disputes, to encourage the digging of canals and the opening of new businesses, sometimes to provide schools, and to furnish a thousand other services too. The national government was not irrelevant to the lives of ordinary Americans, but it was not very relevant either, and the intense factional fights in their local councils and state legislatures often engaged them rather than the more polished debates in Congress. The state and local governments continued on their idiosyncratic courses, responding to the demands of their own citizens and ignoring the pleas of President and Congress when it suited them to do so. When war broke out again with Britain in 1812 President Madison found himself no more able to mobilize men and resources than the Continental Congress had been, and was saved only by the fact that Britain still could not win. In short, the revolutionary gentry had created a constitutional framework in which a national government could legitimately operate, but its functions remained limited and a truly national political society, which integrated Americans throughout the land, had not yet come into existence.

In the course of the 1790s some Americans had their political consciousness raised by the emergence of two national parties, the Federalists and the Republicans, but these were led by the gentry and continued to reflect their preoccupations, particularly their concern with the independence and dignity of the United States. For about twenty years wars in Europe caused anxieties to American leaders, for the belligerents often infringed the neutrality of the United States, for example by interfering with her shipping. Federalists and Republicans differed over how to deal with the European powers, but when the European wars (and the War of 1812) ended in 1815, these foreign problems faded. For this reason, and because the configurations of state politics bore little relationship to these national alignments, the Federalist and Republican parties disintegrated. The gentry had still not succeeded in carrying their national revolution down to the people.

In the end a national society was created but, as Robert H. Wiebe has argued, more because of pressure from below than from above. As Americans spread out across their great land they

Recommended reading

Some knowledge of the history of the American colonies is clearly helpful in understanding the American Revolution, and an excellent recent synthesis is R. C. Simmons, *The American Colonies: From Settlement to Independence* (London, 1976), the concluding chapters of which deal with the origins of the revolution. A brief, interpretative analysis is W. A. Speck, *British America, 1607–1763* (1985), a British Association for American Studies pamphlet. (If the BAAS pamphlets cannot be found in bookshops, they may be obtained from Microform Academic Publishers, East Ardsley, Wakefield, West Yorkshire.) The Speck pamphlet emphasizes the growing similarities between British and American societies, parallel lines of development which may have been a precondition of the War for Independence. An influential social history of colonial America is James A. Henretta, *The Evolution of American Society, 1700–1815* (Lexington, Mass., 1973).

The break with England needs also to be understood from the British perspective, of which Ian R. Christie has established himself as the leading authority, in such books as *Crisis of Empire: Great Britain and the American Colonies, 1754–1783* (London, 1966) and *Wars and Revolutions: Britain 1760–1815* (London, 1982). More detailed studies include P. D. G. Thomas, *British Politics and the Stamp Act Crisis: The First Phase of the American Revolution, 1763–1767* (Oxford, 1975) and Bernard Donoghue, *British Politics and the American Revolution, The Path to War, 1773–1775* (London, 1964).

Revolutionary America itself has been the subject of countless studies. Useful introductions include Esmond Wright, *Fabric of Freedom, 1763–1800* (London, 1965) and Edmund S. Morgan, *The Birth of the Republic, 1763–1789* (Chicago, 1956). The early chapters of

M. J. Heale, *The Making of American Politics, 1750–1850* (London, 1977) survey British, colonial and American political history in the eighteenth-century, though they are already looking rather dated. An excellent, but now also dated, anthology of interpretations is Jack P. Greene (ed.), *The Reinterpretation of the American Revolution, 1763–1789* (New York, 1968).

Essential to an understanding of the modern debate on the revolution is Bernard Bailyn, *The Ideological Origins of the American Revolution* (Cambridge, Mass., 1967), which explains the revolutionary movement largely in terms of the intellectual and ideological perceptions of its leaders. The continuing ideological and constitutional revolution within the United States is the subject of Gordon S. Wood, *The Creation of the American Republic, 1776–1787* (Chapel Hill, N.C., 1969). Also focusing on the ideas and motivations of the revolutionaries is Pauline Maier, *From Resistance to Revolution* (New York, 1972) and, though in a different vein, Eric Foner, *Tom Paine and Revolutionary America* (New York, 1976). Interpretations which emphasize ideology often, although not always, attribute a leading role to élites, and in recent years some scholars have been taking a look at the 'other ranks' and suggesting that social and economic tensions within American society had something to do with the revolution. The best brief summary of this work is Edward Countryman, *The People's American Revolution* (BAAS pamphlet, 1983), and see also his *The American Revolution* (New York, 1985). Since social history often necessarily examines particular communities, some of the more important of these studies have a local focus, such as Dirk Hoerder, *Crowd Action in Revolutionary Massachusetts, 1765–1780* (New York, 1977) and Robert Gross, *The Minute Men and Their World* (New York, 1976). There is nothing new in the idea that the revolutionary war was accompanied and followed by far-reaching social and political change, and the views of a distinguished scholar of the older generation may be found in Merrill Jensen, *The Articles of Confederation* (2nd edn, Madison, Wisc., 1959) and *The New Nation, 1781–1789* (New York, 1950). For some scholars the American Constitution represented either the consummation or the betrayal of the American Revolution, one of the best general treatments being Clinton Rossiter, *1787: The Grand Convention* (New York, 1966).

The American Revolution should not be confused with the War for Independence, but for the military history of that conflict see Piers Mackesy, *The War for America* (London, 1964), Don Higginbotham, *The War of American Independence* (New York, 1971), and Marshall Smelser, *The Winning of Independence* (Chicago, 1973).

An important recent study which carries the American story into the nineteenth-century is Robert H. Wiebe, *The Opening of American Society from the Adoption of the Constitution to the Eve of Disunion* (New York, 1984).